Francis Frith's
CORNWALL

PHOTOGRAPHIC MEMORIES

Francis Frith's
CORNWALL

◆

Terence Sackett

First published in the United Kingdom in 1999 by
Frith Book Company Ltd

Paperback Edition 2000
ISBN 1-85937-229-5

Hardback Reprinted in 2000
ISBN 1-85937-054-3

Paperback Reprinted in 2002
ISBN 1-85937-229-5

British Library Cataloguing in Publication Data

Francis Frith's Cornwall
Terence Sackett

Frith Book Company Ltd
Frith's Barn, Teffont,
Salisbury, Wiltshire SP3 5QP
Tel: +44 (0) 1722 716 376
Email: info@frithbook.co.uk
www.frithbook.co.uk

Printed and bound in Great Britain

AS WITH ANY HISTORICAL DATABASE THE FRITH ARCHIVE IS CONSTANTLY BEING CORRECTED AND IMPROVED
AND THE PUBLISHERS WOULD WELCOME INFORMATION ON OMISSIONS OR INACCURACIES

CONTENTS

FRANCIS FRITH: *Victorian Pioneer*

FRANCIS FRITH, Victorian founder of the world-famous photographic archive, was a complex and multitudinous man. A devout Quaker and a highly successful Victorian businessman, he was both philosophic by nature and pioneering in outlook.

By 1855 Francis Frith had already established a wholesale grocery business in Liverpool, and sold it for the astonishing sum of £200,000, which is the equivalent today of over £15,000,000. Now a multi-millionaire, he was able to indulge his passion for travel. As a child he had pored over travel books written by early explorers, and his fancy and imagination had been stirred by family holidays to the sublime mountain regions of Wales and Scotland. 'What a land of spirit-stirring and enriching scenes and places!' he had written. He was to return to these scenes of grandeur in later years to 'recapture the thousands of vivid and tender memories', but with a different purpose. Now in his thirties, and captivated by the new science of photography, Frith set out on a series of pioneering journeys to the Nile regions that occupied him from 1856 until 1860.

INTRIGUE AND ADVENTURE

He took with him on his travels a specially-designed wicker carriage that acted as both dark-room and sleeping chamber. These far-flung journeys were packed with intrigue and adventure. In his life story, written when he was sixty-three, Frith tells of being held captive by bandits, and of fighting 'an awful midnight battle to the very point of surrender with a deadly pack of hungry, wild dogs'. Sporting flowing Arab costume, Frith arrived at Akaba by camel seventy years before Lawrence, where he encountered 'desert princes and rival sheikhs, blazing with jewel-hilted swords'.

During these extraordinary adventures he was assiduously exploring the desert regions bordering the Nile and patiently recording the antiquities and peoples with his camera. He was the first photographer to venture beyond the sixth cataract. Africa was still the mysterious 'Dark Continent', and Stanley and Livingstone's historic meeting was a decade into the future. The conditions for picture taking confound belief. He laboured for hours in his wicker dark-room in the sweltering heat of the desert, while the volatile chemicals fizzed dangerously in their trays. Often he was forced to work in remote tombs and caves where conditions were cooler. Back in London he exhibited his photographs and was 'rapturously cheered' by members of the Royal Society. His reputation as a photographer was made overnight. An eminent modern historian has likened their impact on the population of the time to that on our own generation of the first photographs taken on the surface of the moon.

VENTURE OF A LIFE-TIME

Characteristically, Frith quickly spotted the opportunity to create a new business as a specialist publisher of photographs. He lived in an era of immense and sometimes violent change. For the poor in the early part of Victoria's reign work was a drudge and the hours long, and people had precious little free time to enjoy themselves.

Most had no transport other than a cart or gig at their disposal, and had not travelled far beyond the boundaries of their own town or village. However, by the 1870s, the railways had threaded their way across the country, and Bank Holidays and half-day Saturdays had been made obligatory by Act of Parliament. All of a sudden the ordinary working man and his family were able to enjoy days out and see a little more of the world.

With characteristic business acumen, Francis Frith foresaw that these new tourists would enjoy having souvenirs to commemorate their days out. In 1860 he married Mary Ann Rosling and set out with the intention of photographing every city, town and village in Britain. For the next thirty years he travelled the country by train and by pony and trap, producing fine photographs of seaside resorts and beauty spots that were keenly bought by millions of Victorians. These prints were painstakingly pasted into family albums and pored over during the dark nights of winter, rekindling precious memories of summer excursions.

THE RISE OF FRITH & CO

Frith's studio was soon supplying retail shops all over the country. To meet the demand he gathered about him a small team of photographers, and published the work of independent artist-photographers of the calibre of Roger Fenton and Francis Bedford. In order to gain some understanding of the scale of Frith's business one only has to look at the catalogue issued by Frith & Co in 1886: it runs to some 670

pages, listing not only many thousands of views of the British Isles but also many photographs of most European countries, and China, Japan, the USA and Canada – note the sample page shown above from the hand-written *Frith & Co* ledgers detailing pictures taken. By 1890 Frith had created the greatest specialist photographic publishing company in the world, with over 2,000 outlets – more than the combined number that Boots and WH Smith have today! The picture on the right shows the *Frith & Co* display board at Ingleton in the Yorkshire Dales. Beautifully constructed with mahogany frame and gilt inserts, it could display up to a dozen local scenes.

POSTCARD BONANZA

The ever-popular holiday postcard we know today took many years to develop. In 1870 the Post Office issued the first plain cards, with a pre-printed stamp on one face. In 1894 they allowed other publishers' cards to be sent through the mail with an attached adhesive halfpenny stamp. Demand grew rapidly, and in 1895 a new size of postcard was permitted called the

court card, but there was little room for illustration. In 1899, a year after Frith's death, a new card measuring 5.5 x 3.5 inches became the standard format, but it was not until 1902 that the divided back came into being, with address and message on one face and a full-size illustration on the other. *Frith & Co* were in the vanguard of postcard development, and Frith's sons Eustace and Cyril continued their father's monumental task, expanding the number of views offered to the public and recording more and more places in Britain, as the coasts and countryside were opened up to mass travel.

Francis Frith died in 1898 at his villa in Cannes, his great project still growing. The archive he created continued in business for another seventy years. By 1970 it contained over a third of a million pictures of 7,000 cities, towns and villages. The massive photographic record Frith has left to us stands as a living monument to a special and very remarkable man.

Frith's Archive: *A Unique Legacy*

FRANCIS FRITH'S legacy to us today is of immense significance and value, for the magnificent archive of evocative photographs he created provides a unique record of change in 7,000 cities, towns and villages throughout Britain over a century and more. Frith and his fellow studio photographers revisited locations many times down the years to update their views, compiling for us an enthralling and colourful pageant of British life and character.

We tend to think of Frith's sepia views of Britain as nostalgic, for most of us use them to conjure up memories of places in our own lives with which we have family associations. It often makes us forget that to Francis Frith they were records of daily life as it was actually being lived in the cities, towns and villages of his day. The Victorian age was one of great and often bewildering change for ordinary people, and though the pictures evoke an impression of slower times, life was as busy and hectic as it is today.

We are fortunate that Frith was a photographer of the people, dedicated to recording the minutiae of everyday life. For it is this sheer wealth of visual data, the painstaking chronicle of changes in dress, transport, street layouts, buildings, housing, engineering and landscape that captivates us so much today. His remarkable images offer us a powerful link with the past and with the lives of our ancestors.

TODAY'S TECHNOLOGY

Computers have now made it possible for Frith's many thousands of images to be accessed almost instantly. In the Frith archive today, each photograph is carefully 'digitised' then stored on a CD Rom. Frith archivists can locate a single photograph amongst thousands within seconds. Views can be catalogued and sorted under a variety of categories of place and content to the immediate benefit of researchers. Inexpensive reference prints can be created for them at the touch of a mouse button, and a wide range of books and other printed materials assembled and published for a wider, more general readership - in the next twelve months over a hundred Frith local history titles will be published! The

See Frith at www.francisfrith.co.uk

day-to-day workings of the archive are very different from how they were in Francis Frith's time: imagine the herculean task of sorting through eleven tons of glass negatives as Frith had to do to locate a particular sequence of pictures! Yet the archive still prides itself on maintaining the same high standards of excellence laid down by Francis Frith, including the painstaking cataloguing and indexing of every view.

It is curious to reflect on how the internet now allows researchers in America and elsewhere greater instant access to the archive than Frith himself ever enjoyed. Many thousands of individual views can be called up on screen within seconds on one of the Frith internet sites, enabling people living continents away to revisit the streets of their ancestral home town, or view places in Britain where they have enjoyed holidays. Many overseas researchers welcome the chance to view special theme selections, such as transport, sports, costume and ancient monuments.

We are certain that Francis Frith would have heartily approved of these modern developments, for he himself was always working at the very limits of Victorian photographic technology.

THE VALUE OF THE ARCHIVE TODAY

Because of the benefits brought by the computer, Frith's images are increasingly studied by social historians, by researchers into genealogy and ancestory, by architects, town planners, and by teachers and school-children involved in local history projects. In addition, the archive offers every one of us a unique opportunity to examine the places where we and our families have lived and worked down the years. Immensely successful in Frith's own era, the archive is now, a century and more on, entering a new phase of popularity.

THE PAST IN TUNE WITH THE FUTURE

Historians consider the Francis Frith Collection to be of prime national importance. It is the only archive of its kind remaining in private ownership and has been valued at a million pounds. However, this figure is now rapidly increasing as digital technology enables more and more people around the world to enjoy its benefits.

Francis Frith's archive is now housed in an historic timber barn in the beautiful village of Teffont in Wiltshire. Its founder would not recognize the archive office as it is today. In place of the many thousands of dusty boxes containing glass plate negatives and an all-pervading odour of photographic chemicals, there are now ranks of computer screens. He would be amazed to watch his images travelling round the world at unimaginable speeds through network and internet lines.

The archive's future is both bright and exciting. Francis Frith, with his unshakeable belief in making photographs available to the greatest number of people, would undoubtedly approve of what is being done today with his lifetime's work. His photographs, depicting our shared past, are now bringing pleasure and enlightenment to millions around the world a century and more after his death.

CORNWALL – *An Introduction*

Crossing the River Tamar brings travellers the distinct impression that they are entering a foreign land. The Cornish have almost certainly fostered this illusion, reminding visitors constantly not only of their county's status as England's most westerly county, but of its unique treasure house of Celtic language, myth and legend. Yet, in reality, Cornwall was only a separate kingdom until 838 when Egbert of Wessex defeated an army of Cornish warriors and Vikings.

Cornwall's perceived 'difference' from the rest of England can be ascribed to several factors: its geographical isolation (its shape has been compared to a fisherman's sea-boot on the foot of England), its hard granite backbone and its ancient mineral wealth. Of even greater significance is Cornwall's strong seafaring heritage - it is surrounded by sea on three sides and nowhere in the county is more than twenty miles from the coast.

In this remote, rocky western land the Cornish have had to toil particularly hard to win an income, for the rocks and seas have given up their riches grudgingly. The fisherman's lot was fraught with danger, and death was always close by as he battled in his small open boat with monumental tides and storms. The Cornish miner, too, endured a harsh subterranean existence, hacking away at the unresisting rock face with the most basic of tools and machinery. Both trades encouraged a toughness of spirit and strong local and regional pride.

John Wesley visited Truro in 1789 and recalls the extreme poverty. 'I could not get through the main street to our preaching-house: it was quite blocked up with soldiers to the east and numberless tinners to the west, a huge multitude of whom being nearly starved were come to beg or demand an increase in their wages, without which they could not live'. Wesley preached to 'twice as many people ... as the preaching-house would have contained'. It is hardly surprising that his dissenting message gained the widespread following it did in the county.

The coming of the railway to the west brought renewed prosperity to the mineral and ore industries, and increased business for Cornwall's ports. The steam train revolutionised transportation, making it possible for many tons of raw material to be hauled quickly and easily from mines and quarries inland to waiting ships. Before the railway, every last ounce had to be carried by donkey and horse and cart along narrow lanes that wriggled inefficiently between settlements. In winter any journey could be an exploration into the unknown.

Cornwall's great glories, however, now seem all in the past. Its fishing industry was once renowned the world over. In the 1660s the naturalist John Ray recounts his visit to St Ives, and records the sheer size and wide variety of fish pursued by the local fleet: 'salmon-peal, ling, codfish, mullet, bass, hake, bream and might, with disused engine houses spearing the skies and the remains of mine shafts, quarry workings and tramways littering the landscape. The county is perhaps now better known for its industrial archeology than its living industry.

Cornwall, blessed with long stretches of golden sand and a temperate climate, had much to offer the Victorian holidaymaker. Tourism was a new phenomenon in the 1860s and 1870s. The Bank Holiday had been established for the British worker as well as annual leave. Working men and women began to

whiting, plaice, soles, turbot in plenty, as also gurnards, red and grey, mackerel, but not many, herrings, pilchards'. In the nineteenth century Cornish fishermen began to specialise, pursuing the great pilchard and herring shoals. By the late 1800s the fishing industry was already in decline, and today, Cornwall's harbours are almost empty of working ships, and its mines disused. Only the quarrying of china clay has continued to expand since its origins in the late 1700s. Throughout the county there is continual evidence of lost prosperity and fallen industrial enjoy days out at the sea. Having helped industry, the railways went on to be Cornwall's ultimate salvation. Passenger services to Cornwall proliferated and holiday visitors were soon arriving by rail at Newquay, St Ives, Penzance and Bude. Local businessmen were not slow to meet their needs. Boarding houses sprang up along the previously empty seafronts and imposing hotels soon crowned surrounding headlands. Cornwall found itself benefiting from the Great British Holiday - a new and seemingly inexhaustible source of revenue. From being modest settlements of simple, often spartan cottages, many Cornish towns and coastal villages rapidly grew and prospered to become sophisticated holiday destinations, renowned throughout Britain.

The Frith photographs in this book depict Cornish life and landscape in all its rich diversity. Many reveal a world in the midst of significant change. Though many of the views show Cornish ports still bustling with vessels, and fishing villages such as Mevagissey, Polperro and Porthleven teeming with boats, the fish stocks had already begun to decline in Cornish seas and the fleets were consequently diminished in size. Moreover, there was the added problem of competition from vessels from East Anglia and the southern ports coming to fish in Cornish seas. We can see, too, that the harbours of ports like Falmouth, Padstow and Penzance are not being used to capacity, and their decline in fortunes is clear to behold. There are also remarkable scenes of Cornwall's industrial past, including the mines at Gunnislake and Camborne and the china clay quarrying at St Austell.

Many views show a more peaceful and secluded face of Cornwall, well away from the bustle of the coast. There are sleepy villages where the country people went about their lives very much as they had done for centuries, and the event of the week was the visit of the itinerant cobbler – see the photograph of Gweek. We see them too, tramping through the streets of their local market town to buy and sell produce, or waiting for the carrier's cart. Today, most of those quiet streets are heaving with traffic. Cornwall's great tradition of church building is evident in many of these placid village scenes. The solid granite churches of Cornwall remain an enduring factor in a changing world. We see their towers reaching up bold and high, visible reminders of the faith, as they still are today.

Cornwall's rivers offered respite from the boisterous worlds of fishing, quarrying and tin mining. The Frith views of tranquil river life on the Fowey and Fal look little different from today – there are ancient stone bridges and fords used by Cornish men and women over a millennium, boats beached in quiet

creeks where the only disturbance is the cry of a gull or heron, children playing in the shallow mud. Though Cornwall is constantly under seige from the many thousands of visitors who invade its roads, towns and villages each summer, it is still possible to trace its unique essence in quiet backwaters.

The many photographs of Cornwall's towns reveal a surprising wealth of architectural splendour. There are fine prospects of dignified Georgian streets in Truro and Launceston, often in close conjunction with slate-hung buildings in an older, more traditional vernacular style. Camelford, Penryn and Helston proudly show their fine Town Halls, dignified and individual, with features that echo more illustrious examples elsewhere.

It is inevitable that at a period when Cornwall was transforming itself into a holiday destination many of the Frith photographs depict the Victorians and Edwardians at play. We see heavily-dressed parties enjoying the sun and sea breezes on the sands at Falmouth, ladies promenading, children playing amongst the fishing fleet at St Ives, a family enjoying a ride in a donkey cart at Carbis Bay, mothers and children paddling at Newquay, and families idling the day away on the rocky shore at Crackington Haven.

THE TAMAR & THE EAST

Travellers to Cornwall must first cross the broad stream of the Tamar close by Plymouth. The estuary here presents a maritime face, with expansive stretches of water that are the province of ocean-going ships and naval vessels. Yet a little upriver from Brunel's eccentric Royal Albert Bridge at Saltash, the Tamar threads a narrower, serpentine course between wooded banks up to Gunnislake. At Calstock it is breasted by the viaduct of the London & South Western Railway. All about is a remote and silent land of twisting lanes and brown stone hamlets. The region was once the heart of a thriving tin mining industry. The combes and slopes around are studded with the remains of old mines and engine houses.

Away from the Tamar the main road to the west is along the backbone of the county, through the mining town of Callington to Liskeard. This pleasing market town has many Georgian buildings and fine stucco terraces. St Neot and St Cleer are two of the many villages huddled nearby on the edges of Bodmin. The country here is rich in antiquities and noted for its fine churches.

Close by the northern edge of the moor is Launceston, the 'gateway to Cornwall'. This celebrated town was once the capital of the county and crowns the dark hill overlooking the River Kensey. Launceston is a place where visitors linger to experience their first taste of historic Cornwall.

South of Liskeard is a country of rolling hills and deep combes, a hidden world of Celtic legend. At St Keyne is a holy well. Legend tells that the Celtic princess, St Keyne, cast a spell on the well, saying that if a husband drank its water before his wife he would be master of the marriage. One unfortunate husband was not quick enough. He rushed to the well straight after his wedding ceremony to find that his wife had already drunk from a bottle she had brought into the church! Cornwall is steeped in such tales, and out of them has grown its treasure house of mystery and myth. South of St Keyne are the twin towns of East and West Looe, straddling a broad estuary. Looe boasts an illustrious past. Not only did the town have a sizeable pilchard fishing fleet but it was in medieval times an important port for the export of copper ore and granite.

Westward from Looe is the celebrated Cornish fishing village of Polperro. Its eccentric lime-washed cottages, many with outside stone staircases, huddle under the dark rocks while, in the harbour, fishing boats thread a path in and out of the breakwaters amidst the cries of gulls.

SALTASH, FERRY AND BRIDGE 1924 76023

For travellers to Cornwall, crossing the broad, sweeping waters of the Tamar deepened the sensation that they were entering a foreign land. Some took the chugging chain ferry, and others rattled over Brunel's curious bridge in the carriages of the Great Western Railway, built in 1859.

CAWSAND, THE BAY 1890 22495

From the village of Cawsand, at the entrance to Plymouth Sound, the seas stretch out to Penlee Point, where the famous hooter alerted fog-bound sailors to the perils of this treacherous coast. 'Cossand' mariners were infamous smugglers in the last century. The spacious bay is fringed with thick woodland.

POLBATHIC, ST GERMANS, THE VILLAGE 1907 57304

The carriage road from Liskeard terminated at this tranquil village of brown stone cottages set by a creek swept by the tides. It is hard to imagine that St Germans, close by, was once the seat of the Cornish bishopric, its church the most important in the county until the building of Truro Cathedral.

CALSTOCK, THE RAILWAY STATION 1908 59704

A modest train of the old London & South Western puffs into Calstock station, having crossed the slender viaduct that bridges the glittering waters of the Tamar. The journey into Cornwall transported travellers into a land of unique beauty, remote brown stone hamlets and the poignant remains of deserted mines and engine houses.

GUNNISLAKE
Wheal Emma, Great Consols Mine 1893

This mighty copper mine scarred the slopes north of Gunnislake on the Devon side of the River Tamar. Here miners blasted the lodes in deep melancholy vaults. The ore was shovelled into trucks and hauled by horses to the surface. The tunnels were lit only by candles stuck to the miners' broad-rimmed hats with a lump of clay.

◆

GUNNISLAKE
The Railway Station 1908

Set at the heart of an ancient tin mining district this pleasing old village straddles the Tamar. The goods sidings at the station recall Cornwall's past prosperity based on the mining of tin. Above the village are the remains of the mammoth mine of Drake Walls.

GUNNISLAKE, WHEAL EMMA, GREAT CONSOLS MINE 1893 32159

GUNNISLAKE, THE RAILWAY STATION 1908 59713

LISKEARD

Fore Street 1906 56300

This busy shopping street reveals a wealth of fine old wooden shopfronts. On the right is Sando's multi-paned frontage and, on the left, a sizeable shop for ladies, advertising its clearance sale of blouses, which is in full swing. Many enamelled signs hang from the fascias, for cycles, oil spirit and dyeing agencies.

LISKEARD, WEBB'S HOTEL 1890 24463

LISKEARD
Webb's Hotel 1890
Set at the centre of a generous open space adjoining The Parade, Webb's was the foremost hotel for Victorian travellers, and was built in 1833 to serve the coaching trade. To the right is an ornate Victorian public drinking fountain, crowned with a gas lamp.

◆

LISKEARD
The Parade 1893
This distinguished market town lies at the head of a valley. It reached its height of its prosperity when the copper mines, at the edges of the wild wastes of Bodmin at Caradon Hill, were working at full capacity. The Parade is a spacious street bordered by elegant late-Georgian houses and stucco terraces.

LISKEARD, THE PARADE 1893 32347

LISKEARD, RAILWAY STATION 1907 58796
Great Western trains thundered through Liskeard bound for Penzance, carrying travellers to within ten miles of Land's End. Here a group of ladies have collected their baggage and wait to board an incoming train. The kiosk is advertising Pears' soap and Lipton's teas.

DOBWALLS, THE VILLAGE 1906 56319
This labourer would not dare loiter for the camera in the middle of the street today. This unprepossessing village, now the home of a major holiday theme park, straddles the main trunk road that bisects the county. It suffers the full impact of constant traffic.

ST CLEER, THE VILLAGE 1890 24471

This placid village hangs at the skirts of Bodmin moor, and is noted for its antiquities. Close by are the Trevethy Stones - a tipsy cromlech supported by six mighty uprights - and a celebrated Cornish cross and holy well, whose trickling waters were said to have special powers to cure madness.

ST NEOT, THE VILLAGE 1893 32357

Nestling among expansive woods and fields, St Neot is famed for its church, with its magnificent 14th century stained glass windows. When St Neot heard that parishioners were failing to attend services because they had to scare crows from their crops he caused the birds to be impounded every Sunday!

LAUNCESTON, ST THOMAS'S CHURCH 1906 56152

This old ivy-covered church stands close by the ruins of Launceston's Augustinian Priory. An old packhorse bridge and ford span the tranquil Kensey river, making it the perfect spot for peaceful contemplation. A grey horse cools its feet in the stream, which is still as a mill pool.

LAUNCESTON
St Stephen's Church 1893 32170
This lane dips precipitously down into the valley of the Kensey and St Thomas's Church. On a rise in the distance is the church of St Stephen. Everyone has turned out for the photographer, the girls in their smart pinafore dresses and the boys in their dark suits.

LAUNCESTON, SOUTHGATE STREET 1906 56130

This illustrious town, often called the gateway to Cornwall, crowns the dark hill that rises from the valley of the tiny River Kensey. It boasts a Norman castle, a wealth of historic houses and a spacious square. The south gate with its twin arches is a remnant of the walls which once enclosed the town.

LAUNCESTON, HIGH STREET 1906 56129

The narrow, twisting High Street is flanked by buildings of all shapes and periods, many hung with the characteristic dark blue slates. At its foot is a glimpse of the magnificent church of St Mary Magdalene, whose granite exterior is lavishly embellished with decorative carvings of quatrefoils, inscriptions, saints and foliage.

LOOE
The Railway Station 1906

In 1872 the surgeon Joseph Lister wrote enthusiastically of Looe's health-giving properties, favourably comparing its climate to that of Switzerland. A steam engine is about to enter the station to link up with a line of carriages that will bring another train load of holidaymakers to this balmy coast.

LOOE
Town and River 1912

This ancient fishing town is divided in two by the Looe estuary. In summer the wooded slopes above are a mass of myrtle and hydrangea. East Looe's cramped main street, edged with a jumble of jettied shops and cottages, tapers down to the quay. Looe's twin towns are joined by a picturesque seven-arched bridge.

LOOE, THE RAILWAY STATION 1906 56395

LOOE, TOWN AND RIVER 1912 64623

LOOE, FISHERMEN 1906 56415

Looe fishermen have followed the pilchard shoals for generations. The town was an important medieval port, and copper-ore and granite were once exported from its quay. These two white-bearded fishermen in their traditional ganseys and oilskins must have welcomed the extra income they could earn by rowing visitors along the coast.

POLPERRO, THE HARBOUR 1901 47794

A thicket of fishing craft take shelter within the tiny harbour of this quintessentially picturesque fishing village, a few miles west along the coast from Looe. It nestles comfortably inside the slate ledges and cliffs of a narrow inlet. Stone-built white-washed cottages huddle around the water's edge.

POLPERRO, THE HARBOUR 1924 76329

Polperro's harbour, dry at low tide, is protected by twin quays. 'Imagine some stupendous giant ...arising out of the sea and letting his axe fall slantwise upon the rocky wall so that it is riven from crown to base.' This description from a period guidebook encapsulates Polperro's unique geography.

Polperro, Old Cottages 1924 76344
Polperro's cottages, many slate-hung and with outside stone staircases, seem to grow out of the very rock, and the town has been poetically described as 'a human bees' nest stowed away in a cranny of the rocks'. This cottage was an infamous refuge for smugglers and a store-house for their contraband.

FROM FOWEY TO FALMOUTH

THE CENTRAL south-facing coast of Cornwall is blessed with safe harbours that protect sailors and ships from the very worst of the Atlantic storms. Unlike Cornwall's more exposed northern coast it guarantees a degree of equable, temperate weather, and is often called the Cornish Riviera.

The prosperity of the region, however, is not based on tourists alone. Around the town of St Austell are massive deposits of China clay that have been worked by the Cornish since the late 1700s. The quarried kaolin is used in the manufacture of china and fine earthenware. St Austell is a plain, workmanlike town with the wide expanse of Par Bay to the south. Quarrying the china clay has created around St Austell a strange lunar region of tips. Around the dust-stained villages of Luxulyan and Carthew is a rich source of industrial archeology, with many disused wheels and engines.

The attractive town of Fowey sits comfortably at the mouth of the Fowey River, which winds lazily down to the sea from the little town of Lostwithiel. The course of the Fowey is punctuated with many muddy creeks, and there are exquisite riverside villages like Golant and Lerryn to waylay the boatman. Lostwithiel was itself once a major port, second only on the southern coast to Southampton. But silting brought an end to its maritime status and it is now isolated from the sea. The river is now used commercially only at Fowey, where great ships weave through the narrow passage between holiday yachts to load China clay brought to the Fowey wharves by rail from St Austell.

Above Lostwithiel are the wastes of Bodmin Moor. Bodmin, Cornwall's county town, was the headquarters of the Duke of Cornwall's Light Infantry.

To the west of St Austell the coast sweeps south towards Dodman Point past typical Cornish fishing communities like Megavissey and Portscatho. Mevagissey boats followed the pilchard shoals, and once landed more fish than any other port in the county. The great fleets are now gone but the atmosphere of tar, nets and lobster pots remains.

This southern region is bounded on the west by Falmouth, which sits at the narrow entrance to the great waterway of the Carrick Roads. Here commercial shipping again rubs shoulders with the holiday maker. The historic port of Falmouth was a vital deep water anchorage, and in the first half of the Victorian era was Britain's Mail Packet station. On the opposite bank is the castled town of St Mawes, now a fashionable holiday resort. Three rivers empty their waters into the Carrick Roads - the Fal, the Truro and the Tresillian. The River Truro noses a path down from Cornwall's cathedral city, by deep wood-ed creeks and past the picturesque waterside villages of Malpas, Feock and Trelissick, their gardens clothed in sub-tropical shrubs.

Truro is the region's glory, with its spacious, graceful streets and fine Georgian architecture. The magnificent cathedral was built in the Victorian era by J L Pearson. The tower was conceived as a memorial to Queen Victoria.

BODINNICK, BY FOWEY, THE VILLAGE 1888 21237
This tiny village straddles a steep slope above the east bank of the Fowey River. Down the slipway beyond the historic Ferry Inn, car ferries ply to and fro across the waters of the Fowey. Bodinnick offers travellers a serene interlude before experiencing the waterside bustle of Fowey with its congested quays.

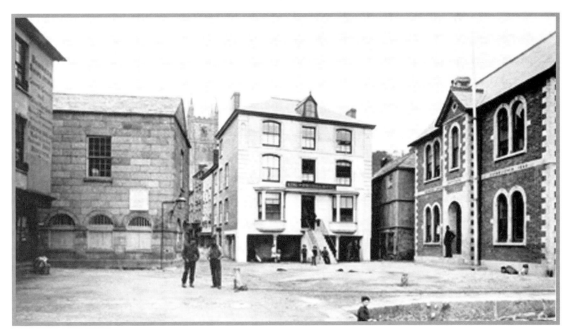

FOWEY, TOWN QUAY 1888 21250

Fowey, the 'Troy Town' popularised by the Victorian writer Quiller Couch, is blessed with a spacious natural harbour, and was once one of the foremost seaports of Britain. Houses and shops cluster about the Town Quay. In the background, behind the King of Prussia, is the imposing tower of the church of St Fimbarrus.

FOWEY, READY MONEY COVE 1908 60911

Though it conjures up images of smugglers, this hidden cove was probably once called 'Redemen' (pebble ford). On the left, a fashionable party enjoys the prospects of distant Polruan from the terrace of Point Neptune House, built by William Rashleigh of Menabilly in the 1860s.

FOWEY, NOAH'S ARK 1908 60920

FOWEY
Noah's Ark 1908
Fowey's straggling main street runs parallel with the river between the Custom House and Town Quay. On the right is the historic house called Noah's Ark, with its twin gables and jettied front. Inside are vaulted plaster ceilings and Elizabethan panelling. On the left is the Sailor's Rest.

◆

FOWEY
Regatta Day 1901
Fowey's most famous son, the writer Quiller Couch, relished the bustle and colour of Fowey's August regatta, claiming there could be no better place to enjoy the bracing sea air. As the yachts tacked to and fro, great vessels slid by with their cargoes of china clay, bound for Canada and the Continent.

FOWEY, REGATTA DAY 1901 47702

FOWEY, PLACE HOUSE 1888 21254
Place House has been the seat of the Treffry family for centuries. It was rebuilt in the mid 15th century, then almost entirely remodelled in the Victorian era. Its battlemented south front is imposing and grand.

FOWEY, PLACE HOUSE, DRAWING ROOM 1888 21255
This heavy interior is typical of mid-Victorian taste, and its architectural detailing presumably dates from the rebuilding of the house in the 19th century. Heavy curtains diffuse the sunlight, protecting the ornately-patterned wallpaper, carpets and upholstery.

GOLANT, THE VILLAGE 1901 47709

Perched among orchards on steep wooded slopes above the Fowey river, this picturesque village is renowned for cider making. In 1863 a railway was constructed along the bank for transporting iron from the mines at Restormel. However, it was soon carrying visitors, keen to savour the joys of the waterside life.

LERRYN, THE BRIDGE 1893 32568

Lerryn must be one of the most perfect places on earth. It stands at the end of a narrow muddy creek, the haunt of the heron and kingfisher, that winds a course between luxuriant woodland. With its old cottages, stepping stones and ancient arched bridge, it possesses a unique, almost hypnotic serenity.

LOSTWITHIEL, THE TOWN 1906 56420

Ancient Lostwithiel was once the capital of Cornwall, and on a slope above the town are the ruins of the 12th-century Restormel Castle, owned by the Dukes of Cornwall. There is much to see in the town, including the old Duchy Palace, the remains of the quays, and the octagonal spire of the 14th-century church of St Bartholomew.

LOSTWITHIEL, THE RIVER FOWEY 1906 56425

In the background is the ivy-clad nine-arched bridge spanning the Fowey River. At one time vessels could thread their way right up to the town quay, and Lostwithiel grew to be second only to Southampton as a port along the southern seabord. By the 15th century silting had brought trade to a halt.

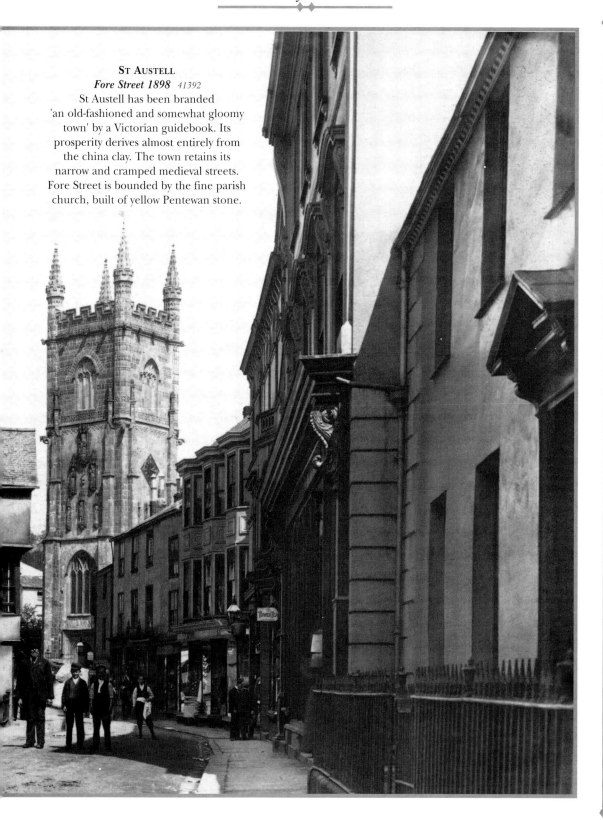

ST AUSTELL
Fore Street 1898 *41392*
St Austell has been branded
'an old-fashioned and somewhat gloomy
town' by a Victorian guidebook. Its
prosperity derives almost entirely from
the china clay. The town retains its
narrow and cramped medieval streets.
Fore Street is bounded by the fine parish
church, built of yellow Pentewan stone.

ST AUSTELL, CHARLESTOWN 1912 64784
A sleek sailing vessel is berthed alongside the quay. Workmen are shovelling china clay down chutes into the hold.
The port was invariably busy, also with cargoes of coal and the sweet-smelling barrel-staves which made the casks
for transporting the finer qualities of china clay.

CHARLESTOWN, THE HARBOUR c1885 16771

St Austell's granite harbour, edged with simple colour-washed cottages, was built in 1791 by Charles Rashleigh for exporting tin. As the china clay industry expanded the port grew in size and significance. Here the bustling quaysides are thronged with ocean-going vessels loading. On the right is a lime kiln.

CARTHEW, CLAY WORKINGS 1927 79869

Cornwall's china clay industry was established in the 1770s. Down the years, pyramids of waste have scarred the landscape above St Austell, creating an eerie, lunar atmosphere. The quarried kaolin is used in the bleaching of paper and calico, and in the manufacture of china and fine earthenware.

ST BLAZEY, LUXULYAN VALLEY 1893 32575

ST BLAZEY
Luxulyan Valley 1893

St Blazey is a modest town that sits inland from the port of Par in St Austell Bay. The wooded and beautiful Luxulyan valley is a magnet for lovers of industrial archeology, with its 1839 Treffry viaduct and aqueduct linking the mining and china clay industries with the coastal ports.

LUXULYAN
The Village 1907

The village is noted for its granite quarries, which furnished stone for the Duke of Wellington's sarcophagus in St Paul's Cathedral. All about are rocky fields and wooded slopes, pitted with gigantic granite boulders. The cottages in the winding street are solidly built of local granite.

LUXULYAN, THE VILLAGE 1907 59359

PENTEWAN, THE HARBOUR 1912 64776

This busy tidal basin, built in 1825, was once linked to St Austell by a mineral railway, and there was also a water-way for transporting stone, ore and china clay to the sea. The fine-grained elvan stone quarried here was once much in demand for the rebuilding of churches.

MEVAGISSEY, THE HARBOUR 1890 27557

Mevagissey's expansive harbour is thronged with boats. Because of the town's pervading odour of fish it was known familiarly as 'Fishygissey'. In the 19th century travellers noted its 'dirt and pilchards' - fishing communities were infamous for the untidy clutter their activities generated.

MEVAGISSEY
The Harbour 1935 86540

In 1886 Mevagissey landed 255,000 hundredweight of fish, the greatest quantity of any port in the west. The twin harbours offered vessels safe protection from storms. The pilchards were cured locally and packed in barrels. It is said the locals hanged a monkey they mistook for a French spy during the Napoleonic wars!

BODMIN, FORE STREET 1906 56279
The county town of Bodmin has a distinguished history, with origins dating back to the time of the Normans. Town lads are lounging on the pavement near the Royal Hotel. The Bodmin postman pauses outside Tickell the tailor's for a chat and, in the foreground, two young sisters show off their new frocks.

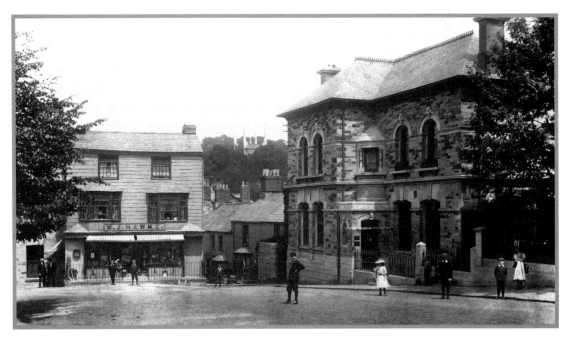

BODMIN, MOUNT FOLLY SQUARE 1906 56278
Delivery boys loiter outside Hawkes' tile-hung hardware shop. On the right is a smart brown stone and granite building, characteristic of the locality. Over the roofs rises the four-pinnacled tower of the parish church, the largest in Cornwall. This broad, pleasing square was later converted into a car park.

BODMIN, THE BARRACKS 1906 56287

Bodmin is the home of the Duke of Cornwall's Light Infantry, which served with gallantry during the Great War. A sergeant major directs the parade. On the wall of the barracks in the background are two targets, presumably for rifle practice. Surely they are a little too close to the windows!

BODMIN, THE PRISON 1894 33558A

This bleak mid-Victorian prison, at the northern edge of the town, was closed at the turn of the century, and quickly decayed into a chilling ruin. It is said that the townspeople relished public executions, crowding the slopes on the opposite side of the valley to watch and cheer.

TRURO, BOSCAWEN STREET 1923 73616

Cornwall's cathedral city is at the centre of a mining district and sits comfortably in a broad valley, at the junction of the rivers Kenwyn and Allen. Boscawen Street, with its granite setts, is at its very heart. At the end are the imposing premises of Lloyds Bank, built on the site of the old Coinage Hall.

TRURO, BOSCAWEN STREET 1912 64732

Truro has been described as 'clean, bright and busy'. Boscawen Street is certainly refined, and its considerable width is due to the demolition of a central row of houses in Regency times. On the right is Heard's Organ Factory, with a spectacular fan of pipes over the frontage. Beyond is the Red Lion Hotel, now sadly demolished.

TRURO
Upper Lemon Street 1890

This graceful thoroughfare of plain, unadorned granite-faced houses was built in 1795, and was considered the wonder of Cornwall. From its junction with Boscawen Street, it sweeps sedately up to the Lander Monument, a Doric column erected to the memory of the two Truro brothers who traced the source of the Niger in 1827.

TRURO
Boscawen Park 1912

A rustic bridge spans an ornamental lake in this picturesque park. Here visitors could enjoy many pleasant walks alongside the river, or sit amid subtropical plants and watch others playing tennis, football and cricket in the nearby playing fields.

TRURO, UPPER LEMON STREET 1890 24132

TRURO, BOSCAWEN PARK 1912 64735

TRURO, VICTORIA PLACE 1897 40593
This bustling scene reveals the pressures for change that beset the Victorian provincial town in the 1890s. This street of small shops is showing signs of commercialism. Edwin Broad, Cash Draper, has overflowed into the next door shop, and just arrived a little further down is an early chain store - Oliver's, the shoe shop.

TRURO, THE CATHEDRAL 1890 23921A

Truro's great glory is its cathedral, which soars sublimely over the roofs. Though it gives the impression of great antiquity, it was built by J L Pearson in the decades between 1880 and 1909 in the Early English style. The central tower rises 250 feet into the sky, and was conceived as a memorial to Queen Victoria.

MALPAS, THE RIVER 1890 24145

The Truro River promises visitors exquisite scenery, its broad banks enriched with lush green woods. Malpas was a miniature port of great antiquity, but is now the exclusive haunt of yachtsmen and weekend sailors. Passengers from Falmouth disembarked at the quay here when the tide prevented a landing at Truro.

COWLANDS CREEK
On the River Fal 1912 *64749*
This tranquil creek, three miles south of Truro, is one of many on the River
Fal. Here two girls are enjoying the sunlight. Behind is a typical ramshackle
scene: a heap of firewood, a tumbling-down boarded building advertising
'good stabling' to visiting riders, and a trio of beached row-boats for hire.

TRELISSICK, KING HARRY PASSAGE 1890 24146
The River Fal is one of the glories of Cornwall, and winds a serpentine course towards Falmouth and the Carrick Roads. Here the carefree rower can potter gently along its numberless muddy creeks, past bankside gardens luxuriant with sub-tropical shrubs.

TRELISSICK, THE KING HARRY FERRY c1955 T209004
The chain ferry offers travellers a fast yet picturesque crossing from Truro into Roseland. At Trelissick is a sumptuously built mansion in the Grecian style, conceived and created by P F Robinson in 1824. Its gardens are renowned for their spectacular displays of azaleas, rhododendrons and subtropical trees.

FEOCK
The Village 1936

A few miles south of Truro, Feock is picturesquely situated at the junction of the Carrick Roads with Restronguet Creek. Its Victorian church, St Feoca, has a detached tower. Feock's original old church, demolished in the 1870s, is noted as the building in which the service was last held in the Cornish language.

◆

PORTSCATHO
The Harbour 1895

This archetypal fishing village was once entirely dependent on the mackerel shoals for its precarious economy. In the late Victorian era it became increasingly popular with visitors, and a row of boarding houses was flung up along its sea front. It offers fine sea views round Gerrans Bay to Nare Head.

FEOCK, THE VILLAGE 1936 87519

PORTSCATHO, THE HARBOUR 1895 37055

ST MAWES, THE RIVER FRONT 1890 24229

This popular sea town sits on the western shore of the Roseland promontory under its castle. Protected from the weather, St Mawes is beloved of yachtsmen, and enjoys fine views over the Carrick Roads. The chapel and holy well of St Maudiz, a Breton saint, gave the town its name.

ST MAWES, THE CASTLE 1910 62884

The castle was built in 1542 by Henry VIII to protect the harbour along with the fortifications at Pendennis and St Anthony. The Royalists held it for Charles I, but not for very long. It is built in the form of a clover leaf, and below the walls is a Tudor block house.

GERRANS, THE VILLAGE 1895 37057

Perched on a windy hill a mile or two north of Portscatho, Gerrans has been called a 'plain-looking village'. The lofty granite spire crowning the battlemented tower of St Gerant's Church was a vital day-mark for Cornish mariners. Though it appears hoary and ancient, the church was almost totally rebuilt in 1848.

PENRYN, FROM THE VIADUCT 1890 24218

Penryn sits at the head of a creek in Falmouth harbour. At the top of the town Brunel's Great Western Railway crossed the broad wooded valley on a mighty viaduct. Here primroses and bluebells grow in profusion in the pretty College Woods.

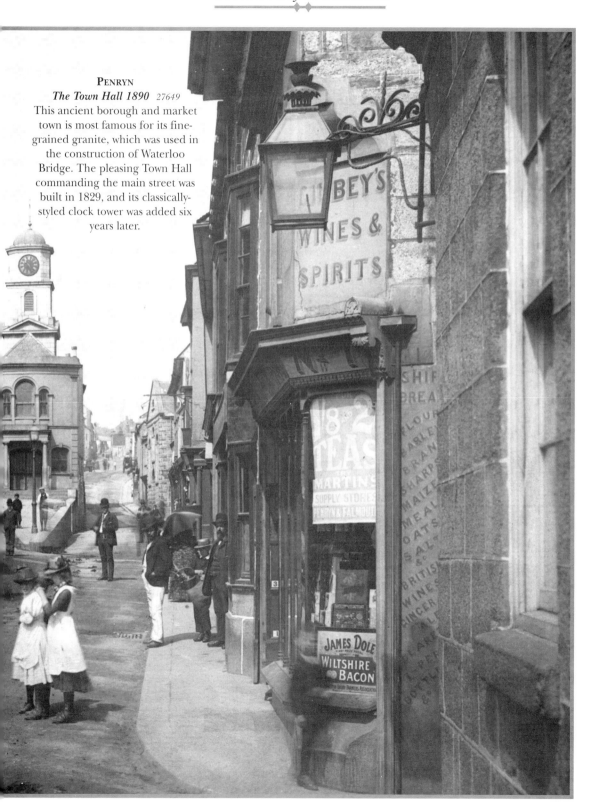

PENRYN
The Town Hall 1890 27649
This ancient borough and market town is most famous for its fine-grained granite, which was used in the construction of Waterloo Bridge. The pleasing Town Hall commanding the main street was built in 1829, and its classically-styled clock tower was added six years later.

PENRYN, HIGHER MARKET STREET 1904 52286

This view shows the continuation of Penryn's precipitous main street as it climbs steeply away from Falmouth behind the Town Hall. Many old merchant's houses here are faced with granite ashlar to bring them a more sophisticated face. Behind, however, they are slate-hung in the traditional Cornish manner.

FALMOUTH, THE QUAY 1908 61059

This celebrated port prospered as a result of its natural deep-water anchorage. The quay was constructed in 1640 and soon after Falmouth was granted the status of Britain's Mail Packet station. From here vessels sailed the world's oceans carrying Royal messages. Here a small fleet of red-sailed fishing boats awaits the tide.

FALMOUTH, JACOB'S LADDER 1924 76615
Opposite the Post Office a precipitous flight of 111 stone steps scales the hill from the town's square to Vernon
Place. It was built in the 1830s by the builder and tallow-chandler Jacob Hamblen to create a direct, if somewhat
exhausting, route between his shop and house.

FALMOUTH, THE BAY FROM PENDENNIS 1895 37031

This vista of Falmouth Bay was photographed from Pendennis Castle. Falmouth was renowned for its equable climate, and Victorian holidaymakers flocked to enjoy its sub-tropical balm. Hoteliers were quick to respond: in the foreground is the new Falmouth Hotel and there are others beyond, including one smothered in scaffolding.

FALMOUTH, THE BEACH 1895 37044

A few visitors peer out at the sun from under their umbrellas. They must have been sweltering from the heat in their heavy dark clothes - leisure-wear had not yet been invented. In the background across the bay, Pendennis Castle sits on Falmouth's southernmost promontory.

THE LIZARD AND THE FAR WEST

TO MANY, Cornwall begins at the Lizard. It can be a bleak, inhospitable region, its coasts buffeted by the gales. Inland, the trees are few, and those that survive are bent double by the force of the wind.

This massive promontory inspires awe for the wildness of its geography, its towering black cliffs and piled rocks, including the colourful serpentine. In the Victorian era, when the first wave of visitors arrived, the local people were quick to make some money from this marble-like local rock. They carved and polished the serpentine to make attractive jewellery and souvenirs.

Huddled among rocky cliffs on the Lizard's eastern flank are the fishing villages of Coverack and Cadgwith, with their white-washed cottages. The coast here is treacherous - ships down the ages have met disaster on the Manacles reef.

The Lizard is bounded on the north-east by the Helford River, which could not present a more different face. Here are secluded villages overlooking the placid water, the haunt of weekend yachtsmen. However, industry is never far away - Gweek, at the inland end of the river, was once a tin-streaming centre.

Inland is sheltered Helston, famed for its Furry Day. It was once an important stannary town with its own coinage hall. Tin has been smelted in these far western extremities for centuries, and at Marazion, near St Michael's Mount, there was once a sizeable smelting community.

Mounts Bay extends in a broad sweep from the Lizard in the east to Lands End in the west. Here is the heart of the Cornish fishing industry. Around the bay are modest fishing communities like Mullion and Mousehole, and others such as Porthleven and Newlyn which once had great fleets pursuing the pilchard shoals. The trade was seasonal, and in July the waters of Mounts Bay were busy with boats from all over southern Britain, competing for a share of the catch. Newlyn was the major fishing port. The lives of whole communities revolved around catching and processing the fish - gutting, barrelling, salting and delivering. Fishing has always attracted artists, and it is no surprise that painters like Stanhope Forbes and Walter Langley came to Newlyn in the late Victorian era.

Perched on a hill overlooking Mounts Bay, Penzance is the region's most significant town. Not only did it have a major fishing fleet, it was also an important stannary town. Penzance grew popular in Victorian times as a holiday resort, visitors enjoying its long stretches of sand and breezy promenade.

Around from the wind-blasted promontory of Lands End the northern edge of this region is dominated by Carbis Bay and St Ives. St Ives has a bewildering maze of narrow alleys and streets fringed with tiny white-washed cottages clinging to the rock. Carbis Bay offers visitors broad stretches of golden sand, and shelter from the worst of the weath-er. It is not surprising the town has become a hugely popular resort. Artists, too, have taken up residence in its cottages and sail lofts to record the extraordinary quality of its light.

Just a few miles separate St Ives from the industrial mining town of Camborne. This plain town of brown stone houses grew swiftly from a modest village into the county's tin mining capital in the late 1700s. One of its sons, Richard Trevithick, helped to create its prosperity by inventing the pump engine that drained the deep shafts of water.

MANACCAN, THE VILLAGE 1930 83192
This hilltop village overlooks the head of Gillan Creek at the northern edges of the Lizard, close by the Helford River. The simple white-washed cottages are grouped irregularly about the church of St Menacca, their gardens bright with red valerian.

ST KEVERNE, THE VILLAGE 1904 53037
Many parishes on the Lizard are rich in ore but St Keverne folk have a superstition that 'no metal will run within the sound of St Keverne's bells'. It is said their patron saint put on a curse on the village, having been treated with disrespect here. The tower is a well-known day-mark for mariners.

PORTHOUSTOCK, THE VILLAGE FROM THE POINT 1904 53041
This tiny fishing village is reached by way of a steep path, and squats in a cove surrounded by rocky slopes. Coastal vessels docked here to take on stone from the quarries at St Keverne close by. The small chippings were used for metalling roads.

COVERACK
A Distant Prospect 1911 64004

The lane winds gently down between stone banks towards this picturesque fishing village of white-washed cottages and bright spring flowers. Out in the bay a mile and a half from shore are the dreaded Manacles, a reef that has been the downfall of many a ship down the centuries. A steamer puffs placidly by.

COVERACK, THE HARBOUR 1936 87513

Life in Coverack was not always as peaceful as this scene suggests. Coverack men were infamous for smuggling, and early coastguards reported that '7,000 ankers of brandy' had been covertly run ashore in the bay in the previous twelve month period. When they were not smuggling the inhabitants fished for bass and pollack.

CADGWITH, THE BEACH 1899 44185

Cadgwith is one of Cornwall's prettiest fishing villages, and huddles between steep cliffs a few miles north of the Lizard. The beach is a clutter of boats and fishing paraphernalia. On the right is the lifeboat house and in the centre a sizeable boat shed, the home of the 'Marianna'. Crabbing is a local industry.

CADGWITH, THE VILLAGE 1911 63994
A fish 'jouster' or seller loads his trap with baskets packed with the latest catch. He will tour the local villages, travelling perhaps as far as Helston with his wares. These thatched granite cottages have turned their backs to the weather and the comfortless winds off the open sea.

THE LIZARD, HOTELS AND STREET SCENE 1895 36223
Many cottagers on the Lizard opened their doors to visitors and sold artefacts made of the local polished serpentine, including necklaces and model lighthouses. In foul weather the Lizard presented a gloomy face, but when the sun shone and the gorse was in flame, it was a paradise for the botanist and holidaymaker.

MULLION, THE COVE 1890 24255
A contemporary guide book offers a poetic description: 'Above rise on all sides hoary, lichen-covered cliffs, rocks piled on rocks, tunnelled, ribbed and groined, with chasms and natural arches, like the ruins of some vast cathedral.' Close by is a magnificent serpentine cavern and, across the water, the rugged Mullion Island.

GWEEK, THE VILLAGE 1904 53046
In the 12th century Gweek was a significant tin-streaming centre and had its own merchant guild. Ancient tin moulds have been found built into the walls of the quay. Its once navigable creek is now silted up. On the left, Mr Courtis the cobbler has arrived in the village in his ornate, glass-windowed coach.

HELSTON
Meneage Street 1924

Helston is pleasantly sited on a hill, above a picturesque valley. It was once a walled settlement with a castle. This agreeable street has many fine old shopfronts, some multi-paned and dating from the late Georgian period. On the left, Wearne & Son's have a fine overhead sign of gilded wooden letters.

◆

HELSTON
Wendron Street 1913

Home of the famous 'Furry-Day', Helston was an important market centre for local produce. Here, country people are awaiting the carriers' carts that will transport them back to their farms and villages. The thatch covering the rubble cottages on the right has seen better days.

HELSTON, MENEAGE STREET 1924 76617

HELSTON, WENDRON STREET 1913 65942

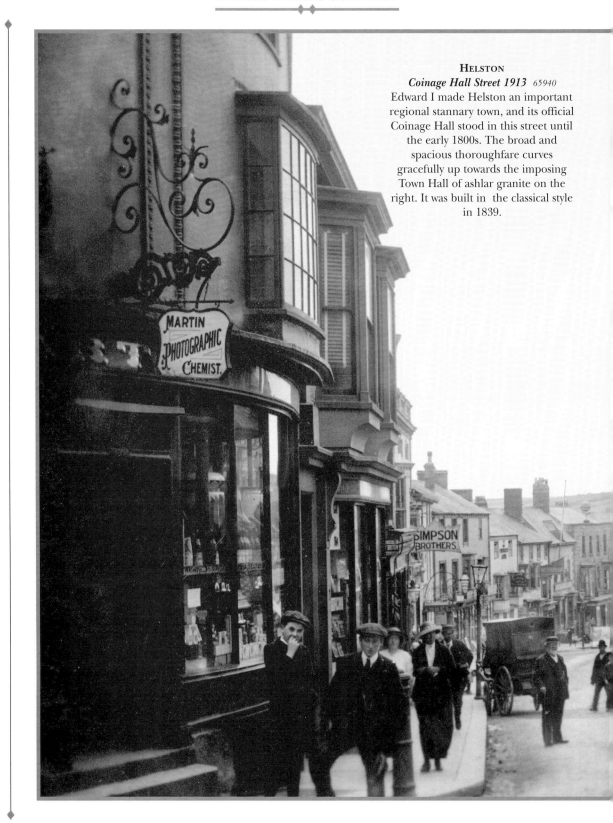

HELSTON
Coinage Hall Street 1913 65940
Edward I made Helston an important regional stannary town, and its official Coinage Hall stood in this street until the early 1800s. The broad and spacious thoroughfare curves gracefully up towards the imposing Town Hall of ashlar granite on the right. It was built in the classical style in 1839.

PORTHLEVEN, THE HARBOUR 1904 52276

This working port is at the centre of the sweep of Mount's Bay. Its stone-jettied harbour was constructed at great cost, but Porthleven has never achieved the commercial success for which it might have hoped. The coast here is treacherous for ships, and in stormy weather entering the harbour can be fraught with danger.

MARAZION, A DISTANT PROSPECT 1890 22997

Described by Leland as 'a great long town', Marazion, close by Penzance, was in the Middle Ages a sizeable settlement of Jews smelting tin. This may account for its older alternative name of Market-Jew. The town was also renowned in Victorian times for its cultivation of a particularly delicious species of turnip.

ST MICHAEL'S MOUNT, NEAR PENZANCE, COLLECTING KELP 1895 36179

This rugged and sublime rock mass is divided from Marazion by the sea, but at low tide visitors can tread a causeway to the island. Once pilgrims came to worship on this mount where St Michael himself is said to have trod. In the foreground men are collecting kelp for use as fertilizer.

PENZANCE, QUAY STREET 1906 56515

PENZANCE
Quay Street 1906

St Mary's Church, rising steeply over the slate roofs of Penzance, was built in 1834. Its pinnacled tower looks down over the old fishing quarter. This narrow lane winds down to the docks and harbour. On the left is the Dolphin Inn and, on the corner, the Harbour Office.

◆

PENZANCE
Market Jew Street 1920

This, the most westerly town in England, has been raided down the centuries by Spanish ships and by pirates. Commanding the broad sweep of Mount's Bay, Penzance grew prosperous both as a stannary town and fishing port. In this street is a statue to Penzance's most famous son, Humphry Davy.

PENZANCE, MARKET JEW STREET 1920 69736

PENZANCE, THE PROMENADE 1906 56510

This breezy walk is one of the finest in the western counties, and promenaders enjoy broad vistas of the sea and boats plying between the fishing villages of Mounts Bay. The Pavilion Theatre, the Alexandra Gardens, and a bandstand are here.

PENZANCE, FISHING BOATS 1890 22978

Cornish fishermen netted every fish they could, but the pilchard was the most crucial and sought after. Huge shoals appeared off Land's End in July and swam along the coast to be taken in seine nets by the Mounts Bay fleets. Later in the year the boats pursued herring, followed by mackerel in the spring.

NEWLYN, OLD FISHER WOMAN 1906 56530

The fisher women of Newlyn clustered at the fish-stalls with their 'cowels', baskets carried on their backs, which were supported by a band passed round their foreheads. This old woman, dressed specially for the photographer, laboured hard to sell her fish, hauling a heavy weight on her shoulders for many hours.

NEWLYN, THE FISH MARKET 1920 69747

The day's catch is auctioned. Though fish were abundant in Victorian times, Mounts Bay fishermen were posses-
sive about their fish stocks. The Newlyn Riots of 1896 were infamous: Four Royal Naval destroyers and a brigade of
troops had to restore order in violent fights between Newlyn men and East Anglian trawlers.

NEWLYN, FISHERMEN 1906 56526

In this contrived but pleasing photograph, local fishermen pose for the photographer. The artists Stanhope Forbes
and Walter Langley settled here in the 1880s to paint the harbour and its fishermen. The town became famous for
its artistic community, the celebrated Newlyn School of landscape painters.

MOUSEHOLE, VIEW FROM ABOVE 1893 31801

The winding road out of Newlyn rounds Penlee Point then dips down to this celebrated fishing village that nestles within stout stone breakwaters. At its back it is fringed by hills. In common with Penzance and Newlyn, Mousehole narrowly escaped sacking by the Spaniards in the 1500s.

MOUSEHOLE, THE HARBOUR 1927 79948

Delightful dark brown granite cottages hug the narrow choked streets of Mousehole (pronounced Mouzel). The village was once Mounts Bay's greatest fishery, and salt was unloaded here from Brittany for salting the Cornish pilchards. Pilgrims sailed from Mousehole's quay to the Holy Land.

LAMORNA COVE 1908 61256
This once beautiful cove, in the parish of St Buryan, was somewhat spoiled in Victorian times by granite quarrying. A quay was built to receive vessels but the dangerous access curtailed the industry. The walk along the fern-fringed lane to the rocky beach is unforgettable. The Newlyn artists were enthusiastic visitors here.

LAND'S END, THE REFRESHMENT HOUSE 1908 61285
In the summer this celebrated granite promontory, England's most westerly point, is inundated with visitors. 'The First and Last Refreshment House in England' doubtless took full advantage of the captive audience. Ruskin saw only disorder in its geology, 'a dizzy whirl of rushing, writhing, tortured, undirected rage, coiling in an anarchy of enormous power'.

LAND'S END
Longships Lighthouse 1893
A little over a mile from shore, this imposing granite tower, 62 feet in height, rises out of a cauldron of furious waves. It was originally built in 1795. The fog signal blasts every half minute. Mariners are grateful for the warning - close by are treacherous rocks including the Irish Lady, the Spire and Kettle Bottom.

SENNEN
The Village 1908
This bleak, wind-blasted village, the most westerly in England, is known locally as Church Town. The low granite tower of St Senana looks down on the first and last hotels in England. King Arthur is said to have celebrated a victory over the Danes by feasting at a rock nearby called the Table Mên.

LAND'S END, LONGSHIPS LIGHTHOUSE 1893 31809A

SENNEN, THE VILLAGE 1908 61281

ST JUST IN PENWITH, MARKET PLACE 1908 61269
This old tin-streaming town is perched on a windy hill a mile inland from the sea. Solidly built of heavy granite, it turns its back stolidly on the gales. On the right of the square is the Wellington Hotel. St Just is bounded by small, irregular fields and stone walls. Close by is the famous Botallack mine.

ZENNOR, THE VILLAGE c1955 Z1001
This granite settlement stands in a treeless hollow, five miles south of St Ives. Though itself unspectacular, the coastline about is rugged and sublime. The Zennor Quoit is a chambered tomb on a wind-blown hill. Seven stout boulders once supported a colossal slab roof, eighteen feet across. Sadly, it was desecrated by farmers.

ST IVES, VIEW FROM ABOVE 1895 35830

St Ives, the pilchard capital of the west and Mecca for artists, encapsulates everything Cornish. With its labyrinth of narrow, pitching streets, its broad stretches of golden sand, its fishing fleet, and welcome shelter from the prevailing south westerly gales, it has been praised as 'the finest spot in England'.

ST IVES, HIGH STREET 1922 72849

In summer months there is an atmosphere of palpable excitement here, as an endless stream of people winds its way down the hill into the heart of the town, turning at the old granite church of St Ia into the bright sunlight of the harbour.

ST IVES, LIFEBOATMEN 1906 56543

The lifeboat house is near St Ia's church. The town was given its first lifeboat in 1839. The crews, usually local fishermen, were courageous but held the sea in great respect. Often, having themselves resolved to sit out the bad weather on dry land, they were obliged to venture out to rescue others less prudent.

ST IVES
On the Beach 1890 24178
Local conditions demanded local design ingenuity.
St Ives fishermen favoured flat-bottomed craft that
remained upright at low water in the harbour surf.
Many Cornish boats had pointed sterns so that more
could be packed like sardines into the tiny harbours
west of the Lizard. The children are on a Sunday
School outing.

ST IVES, THE WHARF 1890 24184

'Its old rickety houses lie nestling on the very skirt of the sea.' It would be hard to find a straight edge in St Ives. Everything seems twisted or warped - the granite setts, alleys and courtyards, blue slate-hung walls, whitewashed rubble, tumbling roofs. Old fishermen sit in the sunlight outside Quick's sail loft.

ST IVES, THE HARBOUR 1925 78658

On the sands the business of the day is under way. Men are gutting the catch and a fish 'jouster' negotiates a price for filling his trap. Soon he will be hawking his wares in local villages, announcing his presence with a boisterous asthmatic roar, produced on a set of leathern bellows.

CARBIS BAY, THE DONKEY CART 1938 81191
Just over a mile separates this popular sandy bay from St Ives. Above the coast path at Porthminster Point lived the 'Huer', whose job it was to watch for the arrival of the pilchard shoals. Here, a family has hired a donkey cart for a ride round the bay

HAYLE, PENPOLE TERRACE 1892 29878
Hayle had no pretensions as a place of beauty. It was described as having 'mean cottages, a few poor shops, an inn and a shabby railway viaduct ... and over all whitewash and coaldust struggling for mastery'. Yet it was a prosperous port and boasted thriving iron foundries and an early copper-smelting house.

CAMBORNE, MARKET PLACE 1906 56433

Camborne grew rapidly from a modest village in the late 1700s into Cornwall's tin mining capital. Its plain buildings of dull brown stone reflect its workaday origins. Here in the Market Square Mr Thomas's considerable stock of hardware has spread out into the street.

CAMBORNE, NEW DOLCOATH MINE 1925 78624

Camborne's massive Dolcoath mine reached a depth of over 3000 feet. To work it economically many thousands of gallons of water had to be pumped out. This was made possible by Richard Trevithick, who invented the first high-pressure steam pumping engine. He was born close by at Pool.

CAMBORNE, CHURCH STREET 1922 73299
The rather severe building on the right casts a deep shadow across this wide shopping street. On the left the display of hardware items has spilled out into the road. The street is a medley of old tile-hung buuildings and imposing Victorian architecture.

THE NORTH COAST

WHILE THE south and west coasts of Cornwall are lively with fishing villages, estuaries and creeks, the rocky northern coast offers mariners precious little shelter or respite. To the west America is the nearest landfall, and these rocky shores brace themselves to take the full force of the Atlantic winds and waves.

Beyond Portreath, where local copper-ore was loaded, magnificent cliffs and headlands stride on as far as Newquay, past St Agnes Head and the sandy bay of Perranporth. At Newquay the River Gunnel has broken through and formed a sizeable estuary. In the middle years of Victoria's reign Newquay was a modest watering-place, with a small dock where china clay was loaded. The coming of the railway created rapid prosperity for the town. Boarding houses and hotels sprang up, and Newquay was soon bustling with visitors, who bathed in the waters of Fistral Bay and explored the rocks under Towan Head.

North of Newquay lies another stretch of forbidding coast, culminating in the great green-capped rocks of Bedruthan Steps, said to be the giant Bedruthan's stepping-stones. It is not until the broad estuary of the River Camel is reached that there is a settlement of any size or significance. On its southern shore lies Padstow, noted for its slate-hung houses and busy harbour. The town was once a major sole-fishing centre and a port of call for ocean-going ships.

The northern bank of the Camel estuary opposite Padstow is the province of the holidaymaker. Polzeath, with its long sandy beach, is sheltered from the winds by the massive bulk of Pentire Point. The medieval port of Wadebridge stands a few miles inland at the head of the Camel estuary. Great ships once sailed past Padstow along the fast-flowing channel and docked at Wadebridge's town wharf. Beyond Wadebridge is a bleak country of isolated villages, many with fine church towers that spear the windy skies and are visible for miles. Anchorages are few and far between, and the bay sweeps north past the fishing village of Port Isaac to Tintagel, legendary birthplace of King Arthur. The scenery here is majestic, with the fragments of the ancient castle clutching at the bare rock, surrounded by plunging chasms and mighty rockfalls. It is a scene that has inspired artists and poets down the centuries, including

Turner and Tennyson.

A few miles up the coast is the rugged harbour of Boscastle, with its long, picturesque street of granite cottages. The harbour is an important, if unreliable, haven for shipping on this treacherous coast. The old rhyme reminds us of its constant threat: 'From Padstow Point to Lundy Light, Is a sailor's grave by day or night'.

North of Boscastle the cliffs continue their majestic course, with the towering promontory of Carnbeak brooding over the rocky shoreline at Crackington Haven. It is only at Widemouth Bay that man once more gains the upper hand. Bude is blessed with shallow sandy bays and broad grassy downs. Before 1900 there was only a modest seaport here, but when the railway arrived Bude grew rapidly to be a major resort town.

PORTREATH, THE DOCKS 1898 41628
At this tiny port, a few miles from Camborne, copper ore was shipped for smelting at Swansea. The village, hemmed in by steep hills, nestles within a deep combe. The harbour was once connected with local mines by a railway - the tracks can be seen on the left of the photograph.

NEWQUAY
The Harbour 1894 33521
An 1859 guidebook described Newquay as 'a small but rising watering-place'. It is hard to believe the town has grown so swiftly. In the late Victorian era Newquay enjoyed brief success as a port exporting china clay. Schooners were loaded directly from the railway link to the docks, built in 1874.

NEWQUAY, BANK STREET 1931 84396

After the decline of its port, Newquay turned its attention to tourism. The population in 1871 was just over 1,000, but by the 1950s it had grown to 12,000. The hills and slopes were soon smothered with retirement bungalows. Bank Street is set back from the front and meets Fore Street at the town square.

NEWQUAY, TRENANCE GARDENS 1928 81278

These civic gardens are in the Trenance Valley and fringe the River Gannel as it twists away from the eastern edge of the town. Here visitors could play bowls or tennis, or simply relax and enjoy the sea breezes. In the background a train crosses the lofty viaduct headed for the town station.

NEWQUAY
Tennis on the Sands 1887
A small party is enjoying a game of tennis on the rocky beach. Despite the warm weather they are sweltering under their many layers of heavy clothing. After the game they will return to their holiday villa, similar to those we can see on the slopes across the bay.

NEWQUAY
On the Sands 1930
This picture shows the classic English holiday. Families paddle in the rock pools, lounge in deck chairs and walk along the promenade to enjoy the sea breezes. In the background terraces have been flung up on the open slopes to accommodate the many summer visitors.

NEWQUAY, TENNIS ON THE SANDS 1887   20251

NEWQUAY, ON THE SANDS 1930   83060

NEWQUAY, ON THE SANDS 1912 64802

Mothers and children paddle in the sandy pools of Towan Beach. On Tolcarne Headland in the background is the Great Western Hotel. The rocky cliff faces are scored and pitted by wind and waves, causing sizeable blowing holes and fissures.

CRANTOCK, THE VILLAGE 1918 68680

Crantock is fortunate to be separated from the brash resort of Newquay by the estuary of the River Gannel, and because of this it has managed to retain its tranquil, country atmosphere. The gardens of the old thatched cottages are bright with tamarisk.

NEWQUAY
Porth 1925

This modest resort of broad beaches and spectacular rock scenery can be reached along the sands from Newquay. Porth Island squats in the sea opposite, and there among the pinks is a blowing hole that discharges a cloud of spray of such size and force that it can be seen from Newquay.

◆

ST COLUMB MAJOR
Fore Street 1922

This attractive little town of slate-hung houses is five miles inland from the sea. The solid, granite-built Red Lion inn, on the left, was kept in the early 1800s by the celebrated wrestler, Polkinghorne. Inside is a minstrel's gallery. The narrow street is now constantly congested with traffic.

NEWQUAY, PORTH 1925 78900

ST COLUMB MAJOR, FORE STREET 1922 72885

PADSTOW
Market Place 1906 56268
You could hardly travel further from London than here, but Williams the Padstow newsagent is displaying the very latest penny dreadfuls. Distinctly lacking in moral uplift, they were of course immensely popular. Hanging on the rack are Ally Sloper's Half Holiday, Puck, Home Chat, Titbits and Handy.

PADSTOW, TREVOSE LIGHTHOUSE 1931 84346

Just west of Padstow is one of Cornwall's wildest and most rugged stretches of coast. Trevose Head juts boldly out into the sea. The lighthouse was built in 1847 with two fixed lights, the highest flashing at 204 feet above sea level. It was powered by paraffin and compressed air.

PADSTOW, THE HARBOUR 1888 21213

For many years Padstow was a bustling sole fishing port. Transatlantic passenger ships berthed here, many built in the town's own boat yards. However, the gradual silting up of the Doom Bar outside the harbour has limited the size of ships that can berth.

PADSTOW, THE ABBEY HOUSE 1906 56269
This 15th-century slate-hung house is on the North Quay and was once the Guild House of Padstow's merchants.
Its owes its name to a legend about a subterranean passage linking it with the monastery that stood on the site of
Prideaux Place, the castellated mansion of the Lord of the Manor.

WADEBRIDGE, THE PLATT c1955 W3008

This medieval port stands at the head of the Camel estuary. Sailing ships from Bristol once plied up and down its channel and berthed at the town wharves. The town has few buildings of historic importance, but the spectacular river scenery and dark green wooded hills make it a popular venue with visitors.

WADEBRIDGE, THE BRIDGE c1955 W3007

At Wadebridge the Camel is so fast-flowing that it is said that there were once chapels on each bank by the ford where travellers prayed for a safe crossing. This graceful but solid structure of 17 arches, built in 1485, must have been welcomed. Its foundations are reputedly wool-packs.

DELABOLE, TREBARWITH STRAND c1950 D21019

To reach this popular bathing cove with its old inn, travellers must thread a path down a deep lane between hills bright with heather and wild flowers. The sea is so pure here it said to offer 'facilities for the study of the sea in its greatest purity, the billows being unsullied by earthy particles'.

BOSSINEY, THE VILLAGE 1920 69653

This village, described in the 19th century as 'hamlet of beggarly cottages', was built around a castle. All that remains is an earth mound. In the late 1500s Bossiney was a rotten borough, returning Sir Francis Drake to Parliament as its member. The village carrier is out on his rounds.

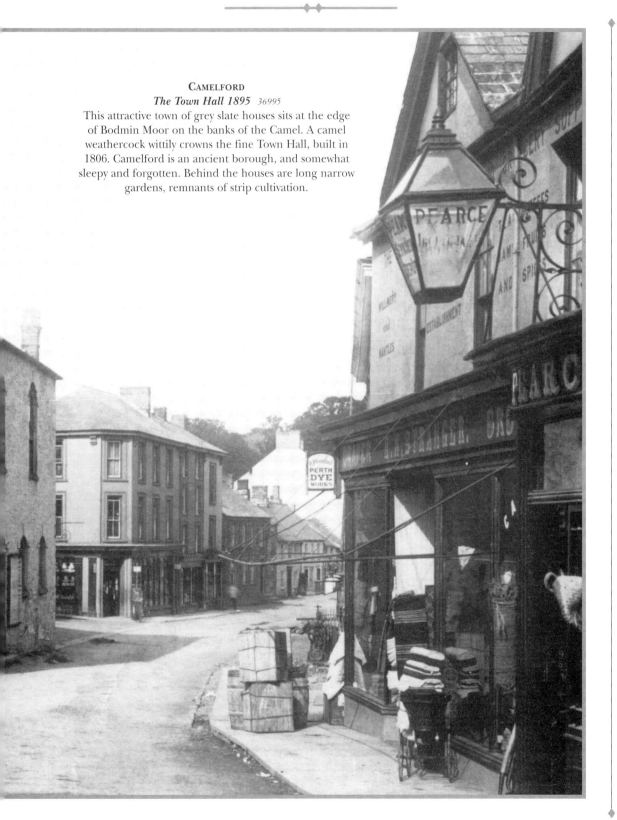

CAMELFORD
The Town Hall 1895 36995

This attractive town of grey slate houses sits at the edge of Bodmin Moor on the banks of the Camel. A camel weathercock wittily crowns the fine Town Hall, built in 1806. Camelford is an ancient borough, and somewhat sleepy and forgotten. Behind the houses are long narrow gardens, remnants of strip cultivation.

BOSCASTLE, THE HARBOUR c1871 5964

BOSCASTLE
The Harbour c1871

Boscastle's rugged harbour is a romantic inlet, twisting and turning for half a mile between brooding cliffs of slate and shale. The sea churns constantly and the cove offers little protection for vessels berthing at the diminutive pier. Hawsers 'thick as a man's thigh' check the impetus of boats entering on the tide.

◆

TINTAGEL
King Arthur's Castle 1894

Fabled Tintagel is the legendary birthplace of King Arthur. The cliffs and castle are sublime, with plunging chasms and precipices, and rough fragments of wall, bastion and gateway bound by china clay mortar. Here, the ragged clouds and the sheep shining in the stormy light combine to create a fanciful, romantic scene.

TINTAGEL, KING ARTHUR'S CASTLE 1894 33595A

TINTAGEL, THE VILLAGE 1894 33602

Situated almost a mile inland from the castle, Tintagel village has a single plain street, a confusion of antique slate buildings and tawdry modern bungalows and shops. On the left, the lumpy roofs of the 14th-century Old Post Office plunge and pitch, the stout chimneys poking at the sky.

BUDE, THE TOWN 1929 82884

With its shallow sandy bays, broad grassy downs, civic gardens, and terraces of unpretentious lodging houses, Bude is almost completely an Edwardian construction. It was once a modest seaport for the Bude Canal but grew in size and importance after the railway arrived in the 1890s.

BUDE, THE CANAL 1893 31893

Built in 1823 to accommodate five-ton tub boats, it featured hydraulic inclined planes instead of locks for negotiating changes in level. By the 1830s, 50,000 tons of sea sand were being transported along its 30-mile length for use as fertilizer on inland farms. The canal was closed, except for the Bude section, in 1891.

BUDE, CHAPEL ROCK 1890 23792

Bude's bay is protected from the brunt of the heaviest Atlantic weather by a breakwater connecting Chapel Rock with the shoreline. There is a legend that there was once a hermitage on this rock. The flagstaff was installed to aid the piloting of vessels in and out of the harbour.

KILKHAMPTON, THE VILLAGE C1950 K18006
This hilltop village, at the head of the Coombe Valley, sits astride the main road between Bude and Barnstaple. It was once the Pilgrim's route to St Michael's Mount. Cottages cluster for shelter around the small square.

KILKHAMPTON, THE VILLAGE AND CHURCH 1910 62406
Buffeted by relentless winds, travellers welcomed a halt at the London Inn. Here a coach is departing. In the background is the tower of the celebrated church of St James. Rich in historic detail, it features a Norman doorway and some fine old bench-ends embellished with carved symbols of the Passion.

KILKHAMPTON
A Corner of the Village c1950

MORWENSTOW, THE CHURCH INTERIOR 1910 62417
This remote church was visited by the writer Baring-Gould. The eccentric Reverend Hawker told him he found it a blessed retreat from the winds. 'Look - without the church - there is the restless old ocean thundering with all his waves, you can hear the roar from here. Look within - all is calm.'

MORWENSTOW, THE CHURCH 1910 62414

Hawker's beloved church is secluded among trees, away from the roar and surge of the Atlantic waves. Here the odd but much loved cleric lived and preached. He kept a 'little shanty' on the cliffs to which it was his habit to retire, to 'be alone with his books, his thoughts and with God'.

STRATTON, THE VILLAGE 1906 56088

Though described in the mid 19th century as 'a poor town lying among hills', Stratton with its narrow streets is blessed with many fine old houses. In medieval times it was a centre for the salt trade. Here, a carter has paused for the camera.

STRATTON
The Village 1906 56089
Over the thatched roofs rises the dark green tower
of St Andrew's Church. It boasts a fine barrel roof, a Norman
font, the old stocks and a ruined effigy of the medieval lord
of the manor, Sir Ralph de Blanchminster.

Index

Frith Book Co Titles

www.francisfrith.co.uk

The Frith Book Company publishes over 100 new titles each year. A selection of those currently available are listed below. For latest catalogue please contact Frith Book Co.

Town Books 96 pages, approx 100 photos. County and Themed Books 128 pages, approx 150 photos (unless specified). All titles hardback laminated case and jacket except those indicated pb (paperback)

Amersham, Chesham & Rickmansworth (pb)		
	1-85937-340-2	£9.99
Ancient Monuments & Stone Circles	1-85937-143-4	£17.99
Aylesbury (pb)	1-85937-227-9	£9.99
Bakewell	1-85937-113-2	£12.99
Barnstaple (pb)	1-85937-300-3	£9.99
Bath (pb)	1-85937419-0	£9.99
Bedford (pb)	1-85937-205-8	£9.99
Berkshire (pb)	1-85937-191-4	£9.99
Berkshire Churches	1-85937-170-1	£17.99
Blackpool (pb)	1-85937-382-8	£9.99
Bognor Regis (pb)	1-85937-431-x	£9.99
Bournemouth	1-85937-067-5	£12.99
Bradford (pb)	1-85937-204-x	£9.99
Brighton & Hove(pb)	1-85937-192-2	£8.99
Bristol (pb)	1-85937-264-3	£9.99
British Life A Century Ago (pb)	1-85937-213-9	£9.99
Buckinghamshire (pb)	1-85937-200-7	£9.99
Camberley (pb)	1-85937-222-8	£9.99
Cambridge (pb)	1-85937-422-0	£9.99
Cambridgeshire (pb)	1-85937-420-4	£9.99
Canals & Waterways (pb)	1-85937-291-0	£9.99
Canterbury Cathedral (pb)	1-85937-179-5	£9.99
Cardiff (pb)	1-85937-093-4	£9.99
Carmarthenshire	1-85937-216-3	£14.99
Chelmsford (pb)	1-85937-310-0	£9.99
Cheltenham (pb)	1-85937-095-0	£9.99
Cheshire (pb)	1-85937-271-6	£9.99
Chester	1-85937-090-x	£12.99
Chesterfield	1-85937-378-x	£9.99
Chichester (pb)	1-85937-228-7	£9.99
Colchester (pb)	1-85937-188-4	£8.99
Cornish Coast	1-85937-163-9	£14.99
Cornwall (pb)	1-85937-229-5	£9.99
Cornwall Living Memories	1-85937-248-1	£14.99
Cotswolds (pb)	1-85937-230-9	£9.99
Cotswolds Living Memories	1-85937-255-4	£14.99
County Durham	1-85937-123-x	£14.99
Croydon Living Memories	1-85937-162-0	£9.99
Cumbria	1-85937-101-9	£14.99
Dartmoor	1-85937-145-0	£14.99

Derby (pb)	1-85937-367-4	£9.99
Derbyshire (pb)	1-85937-196-5	£9.99
Devon (pb)	1-85937-297-x	£9.99
Dorset (pb)	1-85937-269-4	£9.99
Dorset Churches	1-85937-172-8	£17.99
Dorset Coast (pb)	1-85937-299-6	£9.99
Dorset Living Memories	1-85937-210-4	£14.99
Down the Severn	1-85937-118-3	£14.99
Down the Thames (pb)	1-85937-278-3	£9.99
Down the Trent	1-85937-311-9	£14.99
Dublin (pb)	1-85937-231-7	£9.99
East Anglia (pb)	1-85937-265-1	£9.99
East London	1-85937-080-2	£14.99
East Sussex	1-85937-130-2	£14.99
Eastbourne	1-85937-061-6	£12.99
Edinburgh (pb)	1-85937-193-0	£8.99
England in the 1880s	1-85937-331-3	£17.99
English Castles (pb)	1-85937-434-4	£9.99
English Country Houses	1-85937-161-2	£17.99
Essex (pb)	1-85937-270-8	£9.99
Exeter	1-85937-126-4	£12.99
Exmoor	1-85937-132-9	£14.99
Falmouth	1-85937-066-7	£12.99
Folkestone (pb)	1-85937-124-8	£9.99
Glasgow (pb)	1-85937-190-6	£9.99
Gloucestershire	1-85937-102-7	£14.99
Great Yarmouth (pb)	1-85937-426-3	£9.99
Greater Manchester (pb)	1-85937-266-x	£9.99
Guildford (pb)	1-85937-410-7	£9.99
Hampshire (pb)	1-85937-279-1	£9.99
Hampshire Churches (pb)	1-85937-207-4	£9.99
Harrogate	1-85937-423-9	£9.99
Hastings & Bexhill (pb)	1-85937-131-0	£9.99
Heart of Lancashire (pb)	1-85937-197-3	£9.99
Helston (pb)	1-85937-214-7	£9.99
Hereford (pb)	1-85937-175-2	£9.99
Herefordshire	1-85937-174-4	£14.99
Hertfordshire (pb)	1-85937-247-3	£9.99
Horsham (pb)	1-85937-432-8	£9.99
Humberside	1-85937-215-5	£14.99
Hythe, Romney Marsh & Ashford	1-85937-256-2	£9.99

Available from your local bookshop or from the publisher

Frith Book Co Titles (continued)

Ipswich (pb)	1-85937-424-7	£9.99	St Ives (pb)	1-85937415-8	£9.99
Ireland (pb)	1-85937-181-7	£9.99	Scotland (pb)	1-85937-182-5	£9.99
Isle of Man (pb)	1-85937-268-6	£9.99	Scottish Castles (pb)	1-85937-323-2	£9.99
Isles of Scilly	1-85937-136-1	£14.99	Sevenoaks & Tunbridge	1-85937-057-8	£12.99
Isle of Wight (pb)	1-85937-429-8	£9.99	Sheffield, South Yorks (pb)	1-85937-267-8	£9.99
Isle of Wight Living Memories	1-85937-304-6	£14.99	Shrewsbury (pb)	1-85937-325-9	£9.99
Kent (pb)	1-85937-189-2	£9.99	Shropshire (pb)	1-85937-326-7	£9.99
Kent Living Memories	1-85937-125-6	£14.99	Somerset	1-85937-153-1	£14.99
Lake District (pb)	1-85937-275-9	£9.99	South Devon Coast	1-85937-107-8	£14.99
Lancaster, Morecambe & Heysham (pb)	1-85937-233-3	£9.99	South Devon Living Memories	1-85937-168-x	£14.99
Leeds (pb)	1-85937-202-3	£9.99	South Hams	1-85937-220-1	£14.99
Leicester	1-85937-073-x	£12.99	Southampton (pb)	1-85937-427-1	£9.99
Leicestershire (pb)	1-85937-185-x	£9.99	Southport (pb)	1-85937-425-5	£9.99
Lincolnshire (pb)	1-85937-433-6	£9.99	Staffordshire	1-85937-047-0	£12.99
Liverpool & Merseyside (pb)	1-85937-234-1	£9.99	Stratford upon Avon	1-85937-098-5	£12.99
London (pb)	1-85937-183-3	£9.99	Suffolk (pb)	1-85937-221-x	£9.99
Ludlow (pb)	1-85937-176-0	£9.99	Suffolk Coast	1-85937-259-7	£14.99
Luton (pb)	1-85937-235-x	£9.99	Surrey (pb)	1-85937-240-6	£9.99
Maidstone	1-85937-056-x	£14.99	Sussex (pb)	1-85937-184-1	£9.99
Manchester (pb)	1-85937-198-1	£9.99	Swansea (pb)	1-85937-167-1	£9.99
Middlesex	1-85937-158-2	£14.99	Tees Valley & Cleveland	1-85937-211-2	£14.99
New Forest	1-85937-128-0	£14.99	Thanet (pb)	1-85937-116-7	£9.99
Newark (pb)	1-85937-366-6	£9.99	Tiverton (pb)	1-85937-178-7	£9.99
Newport, Wales (pb)	1-85937-258-9	£9.99	Torbay	1-85937-063-2	£12.99
Newquay (pb)	1-85937-421-2	£9.99	Truro	1-85937-147-7	£12.99
Norfolk (pb)	1-85937-195-7	£9.99	Victorian and Edwardian Cornwall	1-85937-252-x	£14.99
Norfolk Living Memories	1-85937-217-1	£14.99	Victorian & Edwardian Devon	1-85937-253-8	£14.99
Northamptonshire	1-85937-150-7	£14.99	Victorian & Edwardian Kent	1-85937-149-3	£14.99
Northumberland Tyne & Wear (pb)	1-85937-281-3	£9.99	Vic & Ed Maritime Album	1-85937-144-2	£17.99
North Devon Coast	1-85937-146-9	£14.99	Victorian and Edwardian Sussex	1-85937-157-4	£14.99
North Devon Living Memories	1-85937-261-9	£14.99	Victorian & Edwardian Yorkshire	1-85937-154-x	£14.99
North London	1-85937-206-6	£14.99	Victorian Seaside	1-85937-159-0	£17.99
North Wales (pb)	1-85937-298-8	£9.99	Villages of Devon (pb)	1-85937-293-7	£9.99
North Yorkshire (pb)	1-85937-236-8	£9.99	Villages of Kent (pb)	1-85937-294-5	£9.99
Norwich (pb)	1-85937-194-9	£8.99	Villages of Sussex (pb)	1-85937-295-3	£9.99
Nottingham (pb)	1-85937-324-0	£9.99	Warwickshire (pb)	1-85937-203-1	£9.99
Nottinghamshire (pb)	1-85937-187-6	£9.99	Welsh Castles (pb)	1-85937-322-4	£9.99
Oxford (pb)	1-85937-411-5	£9.99	West Midlands (pb)	1-85937-289-9	£9.99
Oxfordshire (pb)	1-85937-430-1	£9.99	West Sussex	1-85937-148-5	£14.99
Peak District (pb)	1-85937-280-5	£9.99	West Yorkshire (pb)	1-85937-201-5	£9.99
Penzance	1-85937-069-1	£12.99	Weymouth (pb)	1-85937-209-0	£9.99
Peterborough (pb)	1-85937-219-8	£9.99	Wiltshire (pb)	1-85937-277-5	£9.99
Piers	1-85937-237-6	£17.99	Wiltshire Churches (pb)	1-85937-171-x	£9.99
Plymouth	1-85937-119-1	£12.99	Wiltshire Living Memories	1-85937-245-7	£14.99
Poole & Sandbanks (pb)	1-85937-251-1	£9.99	Winchester (pb)	1-85937-428-x	£9.99
Preston (pb)	1-85937-212-0	£9.99	Windmills & Watermills	1-85937-242-2	£17.99
Reading (pb)	1-85937-238-4	£9.99	Worcester (pb)	1-85937-165-5	£9.99
Romford (pb)	1-85937-319-4	£9.99	Worcestershire	1-85937-152-3	£14.99
Salisbury (pb)	1-85937-239-2	£9.99	York (pb)	1-85937-199-x	£9.99
Scarborough (pb)	1-85937-379-8	£9.99	Yorkshire (pb)	1-85937-186-8	£9.99
St Albans (pb)	1-85937-341-0	£9.99	Yorkshire Living Memories	1-85937-166-3	£14.99

See Frith books on the internet www.francisfrith.co.uk

FRITH PRODUCTS & SERVICES

Francis Frith would doubtless be pleased to know that the pioneering publishing venture he started in 1860 still continues today. A hundred and forty years later, The Francis Frith Collection continues in the same innovative tradition and is now one of the foremost publishers of vintage photographs in the world. Some of the current activities include:

Interior Decoration

Today Frith's photographs can be seen framed and as giant wall murals in thousands of pubs, restaurants, hotels, banks, retail stores and other public buildings throughout the country. In every case they enhance the unique local atmosphere of the places they depict and provide reminders of gentler days in an increasingly busy and frenetic world.

Product Promotions

Frith products are used by many major companies to promote the sales of their own products or to reinforce their own history and heritage. Frith promotions have been used by Hovis bread, Courage beers, Scots Porage Oats, Colman's mustard, Cadbury's foods, Mellow Birds coffee, Dunhill pipe tobacco, Guinness, and Bulmer's Cider.

Genealogy and Family History

As the interest in family history and roots grows world-wide, more and more people are turning to Frith's photographs of Great Britain for images of the towns, villages and streets where their ancestors lived; and, of course, photographs of the churches and chapels where their ancestors were christened, married and buried are an essential part of every genealogy tree and family album.

Frith Products

All Frith photographs are available Framed or just as Mounted Prints and Posters (size 23 x 16 inches). These may be ordered from the address below. From time to time other products - Address Books, Calendars, Table Mats, etc - are available.

The Internet

Already twenty thousand Frith photographs can be viewed and purchased on the internet through the Frith websites and a myriad of partner sites.

For more detailed information on Frith companies and products, look at these sites:

www.francisfrith.co.uk
www.francisfrith.com
(for North American visitors)

See the complete list of Frith Books at:
www.francisfrith.co.uk
This web site is regularly updated with the latest list of publications from the Frith Book Company. If you wish to buy books relating to another part of the country that your local bookshop does not stock, you may purchase on-line.

For further information, trade, or author enquiries please contact us at the address below:
The Francis Frith Collection, Frith's Barn, Teffont, Salisbury, Wiltshire, England SP3 5QP.
Tel: +44 (0)1722 716 376 Fax: +44 (0)1722 716 881 Email: sales@francisfrith.co.uk

See Frith books on the internet www.francisfrith.co.uk

TO RECEIVE YOUR **FREE** MOUNTED PRINT

Mounted Print
Overall size 14 x 11 inches

Cut out this Voucher and return it with your remittance for £1.95 to cover postage and handling, to UK addresses. For overseas addresses please include £4.00 post and handling. Choose any photograph included in this book. Your SEPIA print will be A4 in size, and mounted in a cream mount with burgundy rule line, overall size 14 x 11 inches.

Order additional Mounted Prints at HALF PRICE (only £7.49 each*)

If there are further pictures you would like to order, possibly as gifts for friends and family, purchase them at half price (no additional postage and handling required).

Have your Mounted Prints framed*

For an additional £14.95 per print you can have your chosen Mounted Print framed in an elegant polished wood and gilt moulding, overall size 16 x 13 inches (no additional postage and handling required).

---

* IMPORTANT!
These special prices are only available if ordered using the original voucher on this page (no copies permitted) and at the same time as your free Mounted Print, for delivery to the same address

---

Frith Collectors' Guild

From time to time we publish a magazine of news and stories about Frith photographs and further special offers of Frith products. If you would like 12 months FREE membership, please return this form.

Send completed forms to:
The Francis Frith Collection, Frith's Barn, Teffont, Salisbury, Wiltshire SP3 5QP

Voucher for **FREE** and Reduced Price Frith Prints

Picture no.	Page number	Qty	Mounted @ £7.49	Framed + £14.95	Total Cost
		1	Free of charge*	£	£
			£7.49	£	£
			£7.49	£	£
			£7.49	£	£
			£7.49	£	£
			£7.49	£	£

Please allow 28 days for delivery	*** Post & handling**	**£1.95**
Book Title	**Total Order Cost**	**£**

Please do not photocopy this voucher. Only the original is valid, so please cut it out and return it to us.

I enclose a cheque / postal order for £ . . . .
made payable to 'The Francis Frith Collection'
OR please debit my Mastercard / Visa / Switch / Amex card
(credit cards please on all overseas orders)

Number . . . .

Issue No(Switch only) . . . . .Valid from (Amex/Switch) . . . .

Expires . . . . Signature . . . .

Name Mr/Mrs/Ms . . . .

Address . . . .

. . . .

. . . .

. . . . Postcode . . . .

Daytime Tel No . . . .   Valid to 31/12/03

The Francis Frith Collectors' Guild

Please enrol me as a member for 12 months free of charge.

Name Mr/Mrs/Ms . . . .

Address . . . .

. . . .

. . . .

. . . . Postcode . . . .

Would you like to find out more about Francis Frith?

We have recently recruited some entertaining speakers who are happy to visit local groups, clubs and societies to give an illustrated talk documenting Frith's travels and photographs. If you are a member of such a group and are interested in hosting a presentation, we would love to hear from you.

Our speakers bring with them a small selection of our local town and county books, together with sample prints. They are happy to take orders. A small proportion of the order value is donated to the group who have hosted the presentation. The talks are therefore an excellent way of fundraising for small groups and societies.

Can you help us with information about any of the Frith photographs in this book?

We are gradually compiling an historical record for each of the photographs in the Frith archive. It is always fascinating to find out the names of the people shown in the pictures, as well as insights into the shops, buildings and other features depicted.

If you recognize anyone in the photographs in this book, or if you have information not already included in the author's caption, do let us know. We would love to hear from you, and will try to publish it in future books or articles.

Our production team

Frith books are produced by a small dedicated team at offices in the converted Grade II listed 18th-century barn at Teffont near Salisbury, illustrated above. Most have worked with the Frith Collection for many years. All have in common one quality: they have a passion for the Frith Collection. The team is constantly expanding, but currently includes:

Jason Buck, John Buck, Douglas Burns, Heather Crisp, Lucy Elcock, Isobel Hall, Rob Hames, Hazel Heaton, Peter Horne, James Kinnear, Tina Leary, Hannah Marsh, Eliza Sackett, Terence Sackett, Sandra Sanger, Lewis Taylor, Shelley Tolcher, Helen Vimpany, Clive Wathen and Jenny Wathen.

Free Print – see overleaf